KEVIN

FOLLOW

WALK IN THE RHYTHM OF JESUS

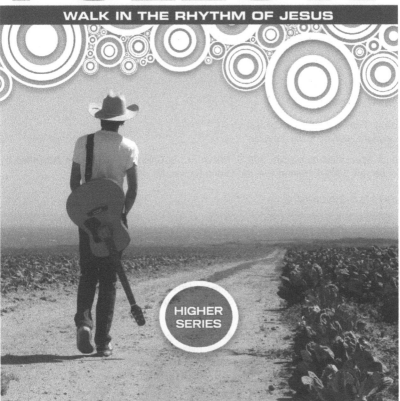

HIGHER
SERIES

T0328042

ZONDERVAN®

ZONDERVAN.com/
AUTHORTRACKER
follow your favorite authors

youth
specialties

YOUTH SPECIALTIES

Follow: Walk in the Rhythm of Jesus
Copyright 2009 by Kevin Johnson

Youth Specialties resources, 300 S. Pierce St., El Cajon, CA 92020 are published by Zondervan, 5300 Patterson Ave. SE, Grand Rapids, MI 49530.

ISBN 978-0-310-28264-8

All Scripture quotations, unless otherwise indicated, are taken from the *Holy Bible, Today's New International Version™*. TNIV®. Copyright 2001, 2005 by International Bible Society. Used by permission of Zondervan. All rights reserved.

Any Internet addresses (websites, blogs, etc.) and telephone numbers printed in this book are offered as a resource. They are not intended in any way to be or imply an endorsement by Youth Specialties, nor does Youth Specialties vouch for the content of these sites and numbers for the life of this book.

All rights reserved. No part of this publication may be reproduced, stored in a retrieval system, or transmitted in any form or by any means — electronic, mechanical, photocopy, recording, or any other — except for brief quotations in printed reviews, without the prior permission of the publisher.

Cover design by David Conn
Interior design by SharpSeven Design

Printed in the United States of America

Contents

Start Here

It's time to let your faith fly HIGHER. If you're ready to take your relationship with God to the next level, this series of books shows you how.

Follow contains 20 Bible studies that lead you upward. You'll find Scriptures that speak to the core of your life, along with space to express what's on your mind. You'll think for yourself and discover significant insights you might not find on your own. *Follow* shows you how to keep close to a Savior you've never met face-to-face. You'll understand what it means to truly follow Jesus. And you'll figure out why being his follower is worth any cost.

Don't rush through *Follow*. You can do a study per day, a study per week, or anything between. Actually, the slower you go, the more you'll gain. Each study is just a few pages long but provides you plenty to think about and act on. The end of each study comes with added material to let you fly even higher.

You'll see that every study opens with a mostly-blank page that has a single Bible verse that sums up the main point. These verses are worth memorizing, as a way to fill your head with the amazing truths of God's Word. Then comes **START**, a brief introduction to get you into the topic. **READ** takes you to a Scripture passage. You can read the verses here in the book or, if you want, grab your own Bible and read the passage there. **THINK** helps you examine the main ideas of the text, and **LIVE** makes it easy to apply what you learn. **WRAP** pulls everything together.

Then there's some bonus material. **MORE THOUGHTS TO MULL** tosses you a few more questions to ask yourself or others. **MORE SCRIPTURES TO DIG** leads you to related Bible passages to help you hear even more from God on the topic.

Whether you read on your own or get together with a group, *Follow* will help your faith fly high. It will lead you closer to Jesus and help you walk in his rhythm, living more and more like him in your everyday world.

Kevin Johnson

1. THE MAIN THING

Why Jesus showed up on earth

Matthew 1:21

"You are to give him the name Jesus, because he will save his people from their sins."

START The Bible's bold portrait of Jesus should astonish us—even if we've heard the Christmas story hundreds of times. More than two thousand years ago in the ancient Middle East, a baby boy came screaming into the world like any other child. Yet angels sang at his birth. Shepherds ran from their fields to greet him. Wise astronomers brought him rare gifts and knelt before him as King. Yet even more extraordinary were the facts that would unfold in time: Jesus is God in human form. He came to save the world. And he wants the whole human race to follow him.

From his birth to his life, death, and resurrection, Jesus astounded the world. Based on what you know about Jesus right now, what do you think about him?

READ Matthew 1:18-21

> [18]This is how the birth of Jesus the Messiah came about: His mother Mary was pledged to be married to Joseph, but before they came together, she was found to be pregnant through the Holy Spirit. [19]Because Joseph her husband was a righteous man and did not want to expose her to public disgrace, he had in mind to divorce her quietly.
>
> [20]But after he had considered this, an angel of the Lord appeared to him in a dream and said, "Joseph son of David, do not be afraid to take Mary home as your wife, because what is conceived in her is from the Holy Spirit. [21]She will give birth to a son, and you are to give him the name Jesus, because he will save his people from their sins."

THINK When Joseph learned Mary was pregnant, he couldn't help but assume she had cheated on him. Her unfaithfulness could have been punished with death by stoning, and the couple's strict "betrothal" required a divorce to break. But where does Mary's baby come from?

Some ancient religious writings depict gods having sex, but that's not the picture here. The "virgin birth" (or "virgin conception") of Jesus is a miraculous act of God, a powerful intervention in the world he created and controls. Hundreds of years before Jesus was born, this event was predicted by the Old Testament prophet Isaiah: "The virgin will conceive and give birth to a son" (Isaiah 7:14). Jesus is more than a human child. He is "the Son of the Most High" (Luke 1:32).

Why did Jesus come to earth? What would he accomplish?

Don't miss the deep meaning here: The angel tells Joseph to name the child "Jesus" (*Iesous* in New Testament Greek), a form of the name "Joshua," which means "Yahweh (God) saves."

LIVE Why does it matter that Jesus was born to a virgin? What does that tell you about who he is?

The arrival of Jesus assumes that you and the rest of the human race need a Savior. Do you agree—or disagree? Why?

God sent a baby to rescue you. Good idea—or not? How come?

WRAP Jesus didn't show up on earth as a fully-formed hero of the world. Before he could save humanity, he would experience life just as we do (Hebrews 4:14-16) and learn from everything he suffered (Hebrews 2:10). Yet right from the start Jesus was nothing less than God's Son, the Savior of the world.

» MORE THOUGHTS TO MULL

- What do you think the human race needs to be saved from the most?

- If you were God and wanted to send a rescuer to earth, who would you send?

- The early Christians who recorded the events of Jesus' life wanted people in all places and times to believe their message. How would the extraordinary circumstances surrounding Jesus' birth have helped their cause—or hurt it? Explain.

» MORE SCRIPTURES TO DIG

- Jesus was a miracle baby, the Son of God conceived by the power of the Holy Spirit within Mary, a virgin. See this event through his mom's eyes in **Luke 1:32-35**.

- Read **Matthew 1:24-25**, which tells how Joseph heard the news that his virgin bride-to-be was pregnant with a very important child. You'll catch his biological bewilderment, his tender care for Mary, and his clear obedience to God.

- The people of Israel expected their Savior to be an earthly king, a mighty political leader who would drive out the Romans who occupied their land. While the Savior might have been difficult to spot as a baby, **Matthew 1:21-23** says angels proclaimed who Jesus truly was: He is Immanuel ("God with us") and Jesus ("the Lord saves").

- The Bible doesn't say much about Jesus' childhood. He was born in Bethlehem (**Luke 2:1-20**), brought to the temple (**Luke 2:21-40**), visited by Magi from the east (**Matthew 2:1-12**), and fled to Egypt to escape the murderous King Herod (**Matthew 2:13-18**). He grew up in Nazareth (**Matthew 2:19-23**), and as a young teen, he stumped the land's foremost religious teachers (**Luke 2:41-50**). **Luke 2:52** sums up this period: "Jesus became wiser and grew physically. People liked him, and he pleased God" (NCV).

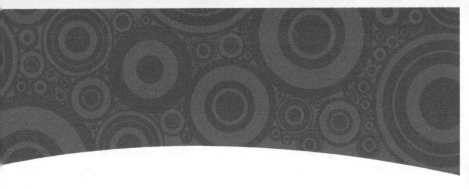

2. OPENING ACT

Spot the world's Savior

Luke 4:20-21

Then he rolled up the scroll, gave it back to the attendant and sat down. The eyes of everyone in the synagogue were fastened on him. He began by saying to them, "Today this scripture is fulfilled in your hearing."

START Hundreds of years before the baby Jesus was born in Bethlehem, the Old Testament detailed what the world could expect of this one-of-a-kind Savior: "For to us a child is born, to us a son is given, and the government will be on his shoulders. And he will be called Wonderful Counselor, Mighty God, Everlasting Father, Prince of Peace. Of the increase of his government and peace there will be no end. He will reign on David's throne and over his kingdom, establishing and upholding it with justice and righteousness from that time on and forever. The zeal of the Lord Almighty will accomplish this" (Isaiah 9:6-7).

That's a partial job description of the Savior that God promised to send. Describe in half a dozen words what this Redeemer will be like.

READ Luke 4:14-21

[14]Jesus returned to Galilee in the power of the Spirit, and news about him spread through the whole countryside. [15]He was teaching in their synagogues, and everyone praised him.

[16]He went to Nazareth, where he had been brought up, and on the Sabbath day he went into the synagogue, as was his custom. He stood up to read, [17]and the scroll of the prophet Isaiah was handed to him. Unrolling it, he found the place where it is written:

[18]"The Spirit of the Lord is on me, because he has anointed me to proclaim good news to the poor.

He has sent me to proclaim freedom for the prisoners and recovery of sight for the blind,

to set the oppressed free, [19]to proclaim the year of the Lord's favor."

[20]Then he rolled up the scroll, gave it back to the attendant and sat down. The eyes of everyone in the synagogue were fastened on him. [21]He began by saying to them, "Today this scripture is fulfilled in your hearing."

THINK When Jesus shows up in his hometown synagogue—the local Jewish assembly—people in the surrounding area have already begun to take note of the power of what he said and did. The passage Jesus reads from Isaiah 61:1-2 is yet another description of the Savior that God promised to send. What will this Savior do?

This Bible doesn't say whether the passage Jesus read was scheduled for that day or picked by Jesus. Either way, he uses the occasion to make an enormous claim. And his sitting down after completing the reading doesn't mean he's done. It signals his readiness to teach. So what does Jesus declare to all his townsfolk?

All the people who hear Jesus realize that he was reading a Scripture about the Savior that God promised to send. They grasp that Jesus is claiming to be the fulfillment of the promise. Moments later their applause turns to anger, and the lifelong neighbors of Jesus attempt to toss him off a cliff (Luke 4:22-30).

LIVE Why would the people from the town where Jesus grew up turn on him?

As you ponder the kind of Savior Jesus promises to be (one who declares good news to the poor, frees captives, heals the blind, frees the oppressed, and declares God's gracious care) are you intrigued...or unimpressed...or irritated? What do you feel—and why?

Why would God reveal details about Jesus before he arrives?

WRAP The dozens of Old Testament prophecies about the Savior—see "More Scriptures to Dig" below—helped people recognize the Savior that God was sending. He would be God's "Messiah" or "Christ," one who is "anointed" or "chosen." When it comes to Jesus, the promises aren't empty words. The more you learn about Jesus, the more you see him living up to these incredible predictions.

≫   MORE THOUGHTS TO MULL

- Suppose you could write a job description for a hero to fix everything wrong in the world. What would you put at the top of that person's to-do list?

- How is the Old Testament an indispensable part of understanding Jesus?

- How do you know Jesus didn't just arrange his life to fulfill all the prophecies of the Old Testament?

≫   MORE SCRIPTURES TO DIG

- After Jesus rose from the dead, he used his fulfillment of Old Testament prophecies to explain who he was and why he came. Check the conversation in **Luke 24:13-32**.

- Anyone could claim to be the Messiah promised in the Old Testament. But it's truly astounding that there are dozens of predictions that came true in the New Testament through Jesus—details accurately foretold hundreds of years before his arrival, most of them completely beyond his control. Here are just a few of these Bible prophecies:

PREDICTED IN THE OLD TESTAMENT	FULFILLED IN JESUS
The Savior would...	
be a descendant of King David 2 Samuel 7:12	Matthew 1:1
be born in the town of Bethlehem Micah 5:2-5	Luke 2:4-7
heal the sick Isaiah 35:5-6	Matthew 11:5
be beaten for no reason Psalm 69:4	John 15:24-25

PREDICTED IN THE OLD TESTAMENT	FULFILLED IN JESUS
The Savior would...	
be silent before his accusers	
Isaiah 53:7	Matthew 27:12-14
be pierced in his side	
Zechariah 12:10	John 19:34
rise from the dead	
Psalm 16:10	Mark 16:6

Other Bible prophecies reveal even more detail about God's servant, yet there's one point you don't want to miss. **Isaiah 53:5** foretold that God would send a Savior who would die the death each person deserves: "He was pierced for our transgressions, he was crushed for our iniquities; the punishment that brought us peace was upon him, and by his wounds we are healed."

3. DROP AND GO

Invited to follow Jesus

Matthew 4:19-20

"Come, follow me," Jesus said, "and I will send you out to fish for people." At once they left their nets and followed him.

START You might think that when the first disciples left everything behind to follow Jesus, they were rushing off to serve a guy they knew nothing about—as if they'd been lured into following him by an eerie stare. But the Bible serves up obvious clues that the earliest followers of Jesus knew who was asking them to drop everything and run after him. For example, when we read in Mark 2:13-14 about a tax collector named Levi who decides to follow, we know from the previous chapter that Jesus had been teaching and doing miracles in the area, and news about him had already spread far and wide (Mark 1:28). And the fishermen who follow Jesus in the passage below? An account early in the book of John shows this wasn't the first time they had met Jesus.

How would you respond if Jesus walked up to you and said, "Drop everything! Follow me! Now!"?

READ Matthew 4:18-23

> [18]As Jesus was walking beside the Sea of Galilee, he saw two brothers, Simon called Peter and his brother Andrew. They were casting a net into the lake, for they were fishermen. [19]"Come, follow me," Jesus said, "and I will send you out to fish for people." [20]At once they left their nets and followed him.
>
> [21]Going on from there, he saw two other brothers, James son of Zebedee and his brother John. They were in a boat with their father Zebedee, preparing their nets. Jesus called them, [22]and immediately they left the boat and their father and followed him.
>
> [23]Jesus went throughout Galilee, teaching in their synagogues, proclaiming the good news of the kingdom, and healing every disease and sickness among the people.

THINK These early disciples—Peter, Andrew, James, and John—have heard enough about Jesus to understand a bit of who he is (see their encounter with him in John 1:35-51). Still, their decision to drop everything and follow him is startling. How do these guys respond when Jesus invites them to follow him?

What does Jesus want Peter and Andrew to do? What does that mean?

Once these disciples take off after Jesus, what kinds of things do they hear Jesus say and watch him do? What would that have been like?

LIVE How do you think Jesus invites people to follow him today? How can you respond to his call?

Who has an easier time following Jesus—us or the people back in the Bible? Explain your answer.

Jesus invites you to go where he goes...to be with him...to do the good he does...to ditch the evil he refuses to be part of. What habits, friendships, or possessions get in the way of you following him wholeheartedly? What else might hold you back?

WRAP Jesus doesn't expect you to follow him without figuring out the basics of who he is and what he expects of you—and the more you grasp the facts about Jesus, the more you'll know why he's worth following. But don't dawdle. The early followers of Jesus did what they knew they needed to do. They dropped their nets. Right away. No hesitation.

≫   MORE THOUGHTS TO MULL

- What do you think the father of James and John thought when his sons left him in the middle of preparing their nets for a fishing expedition?

- When have you sensed Jesus inviting you to follow him—to know him better and hang tighter with him? How did you respond?

- Is Jesus the kind of leader who *demands* respect—or *commands* respect by inspiring others to follow after him? Explain your answer.

» MORE SCRIPTURES TO DIG

- You can read about Jesus' calling his early disciples elsewhere in the Gospels: **Mark 1:16-20**, **Luke 5:2-11**, and **John 1:35-42**.

- Not everyone back in Bible times chose to follow Jesus, even after a personal invitation from the Savior himself. See a concrete example in the "rich young ruler," whose attachment to his wealth caused him to turn away from Jesus (**Luke 18:18-25**).

- Once after an especially tough-to-understand teaching by Jesus "many of his followers left him and stopped following him" (**John 6:66**, NCV). Those who stayed had reached the conclusion that Jesus was still everything he claimed to be. When Jesus asked his twelve closest friends, "Do you want to leave, too?" Peter answered for the rest: "Lord, who would we go to? You have the words that give eternal life. We believe and know that you are the Holy One from God" (**John 6:68-69**, NCV).

- Jesus invited us to think hard about the cost of following him. Look at **Luke 14:25-33**.

4. CALL OF THE WILD

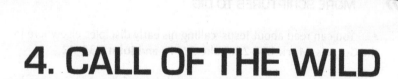

Jesus wants imperfect people

Luke 5:27-28

After this, Jesus went out and saw a tax collector by the name of Levi sitting at his tax booth. "Follow me," Jesus said to him, and Levi got up, left everything and followed him.

START When Jesus went looking for his first disciples, he didn't criss-cross the nation and choose the most promising followers through an endless string of talent auditions. He didn't hunt for the brightest or the most beautiful or the best behaved. Truth is, his picks look surprisingly average. Or way below average. Or even downright notorious.

READ Luke 5:27-32

> ²⁷After this, Jesus went out and saw a tax collector by the name of Levi sitting at his tax booth. "Follow me," Jesus said to him, ²⁸and Levi got up, left everything and followed him.
>
> ²⁹Then Levi held a great banquet for Jesus at his house, and a large crowd of tax collectors and others were eating with them. ³⁰But the Pharisees and the teachers of the law who belonged to their sect complained to his disciples, "Why do you eat and drink with tax collectors and sinners?"
>
> ³¹Jesus answered them, "It is not the healthy who need a doctor, but the sick. ³²I have not come to call the righteous, but sinners to repentance."

THINK Levi is another name for Matthew (Matthew 9:9), the disciple who wrote the first book of the New Testament. What does Levi do for a living? Why mention his occupation?

Tax collectors were despised not only for cheating their fellow citizens but also for collaborating with hated Roman rulers. They were among the ultimate examples of sinful outcasts, often mentioned along with prostitutes and other major evildoers. Yet Jesus deliberately includes a tax collector among his twelve closest friends.

Levi responds eagerly to Jesus' command to get up and go, then throws a giant party. Who does Levi invite? Why them?

Don't miss two facts: Levi doesn't hide Jesus from people who might think he's uncool, and Jesus makes quick friends with a mass of people that others regard as hopeless.

Who gets irate with Jesus for dining with all of these "tax collectors and sinners"? How come?

LIVE It might be tough to picture the Son of God hanging out with a crowd of cheats, drunks, and prostitutes. Yet he does. Is Jesus making a good choice— or not? Explain.

To the religious rulers, eating with sinners was nearly as bad as actually doing an evil deed, and making friends with sinners meant you were thoroughly evil. Jesus utters some well-known words to silence these critics. Sum up in your own words what he says.

Imagine yourself back in this Bible scene. Are you inside with Jesus and the sinners—or outside with the religious folk? Why?

WRAP Jesus isn't looking for perfect people. In fact his point was that all of us are imperfect—sinful wrongdoers desperately needing his help. Like the Bible says, "There is no one righteous, not even one" (Romans 3:10) and "Everyone has sinned; we all fall short of God's glorious standard" (Romans 3:23, NLT). Jesus wants the whole world to follow him. Yet to get up and run after him you have to admit you need his help.

» MORE THOUGHTS TO MULL

- Why does Jesus go looking for imperfect people?

- What do you think Jesus did—and didn't do—as he hung out with the sinful outcasts of his society?

- Who is more sinful—the "tax collectors and sinners" or the Pharisees and other religious folk? Explain.

- What keeps you from admitting your imperfection—and your need for Jesus?

» MORE SCRIPTURES TO DIG

- There's a Sunday school song that starts "Zacchaeus was a wee little man...." Like Levi, Zacchaeus was a tax collector. Read about him in **Luke 19:1-10.** Don't miss how Zach responds to Jesus—and Jesus' end-of-the-passage explanation of his own actions.

- When you hear the word *disciples*, you might think only of the twelve followers Jesus chose to be with him all the time (**Luke 6:12-15**). The word *disciple*, however, applies to anyone who follows Jesus, not only the larger band that trekked with Jesus but also *you*. Jesus also called his inner twelve "apostles," people given a special job of spreading his message.

- Following Jesus isn't an optional part of being a Christian. In **John 12:26** Jesus said, "Whoever serves me must follow me; and where I am, my servant also will be."

5. ABOVE THE CROWD

Test the truth of Jesus' words

John 7:17 (NLT)

"Anyone who wants to do the will of God will know whether my teaching is from God or is merely my own."

START A hundred times a day we bump into opinions and perspectives—alternative points of view held by friends, enemies, parents, teachers, advertisers, and a world of others. Jesus claims his words are how we can get a grip on reality and experience the one real God. His voice, he says, is worth listening to above the roar of the crowd.

You can't deny that a multitude of voices battle for your attention. Whose words do you trust most of all? Why?

READ John 7:16-18 (NLT)

> [16]So Jesus told them, "My message is not my own; it comes from God who sent me. [17]Anyone who wants to do the will of God will know whether my teaching is from God or is merely my own. [18]Those who speak for themselves want glory only for themselves, but a person who seeks to honor the one who sent him speaks truth, not lies.

THINK This passage catches Jesus in a confrontation during a major Jewish feast. The crowds are awed by his powerful message, but the religious leaders are plotting to kill him. Where does Jesus say his teaching comes from?

Jesus is God, yet he makes a clear distinction between himself and God the Father. Jesus is more than a mouthpiece. He and the Father speak with such unity that the Son's words perfectly reflect the Father's message.

How can people be certain they can rely on Jesus' teaching?

What does it mean to "want to do the will of God"?

That desire to do God's will isn't a feeble "Maybe I will—or maybe I won't." Wanting to do God's will is a settled choice, a rock-solid determination to obey God's commands and follow his plan for your life.

If you commit yourself to doing God's will, what does Jesus say you'll know about his teaching?

LIVE Jesus says he differs from other voices who "speak for themselves," presenting their own ideas. What motivates people to shout into your life? What motivates Jesus?

In what areas of life do you have a tough time trusting Jesus' words—either relying on his promises or doing his commands?

Based on your last answer, can you expect Jesus' words to be reliable? How real does Jesus seem to you?

WRAP When it comes to the teachings of Jesus, you can't guess from a distance whether they're true or not. He wants you to wrap your life around his words, trusting that he speaks truth, trying his teachings for yourself. If you do, you will know his words come straight from heaven.

» MORE THOUGHTS TO MULL

- Is it fair that Jesus expects you to try out his words before you can fully grasp their truthfulness? Why—or why not?

- Why do some people choose to distrust Jesus as their ultimate source of truth?

- Who do you know who takes Jesus and his words seriously? Ask those people why they listen so attentively to Jesus.

»   MORE SCRIPTURES TO DIG

- Read all of **John 7** to see this whole scene of people reacting to Jesus and his words. The confrontation starts when Jesus slips into Jerusalem, then stands in the temple to preach. He challenges everyone to put his words into practice, including the religious leaders who oppose him and plot to kill him. Some people there wonder aloud if Jesus is the Christ, the Messiah sent by God. The chapter ends with a phenomenal promise of satisfaction for all who truly try Jesus (**John 7:37-39**).

- In **John 17:17** Jesus tells the Father, "Your word is truth." Check **Ephesians 1:13** and **Colossians 1:5**, which describe the "word of truth" as nothing less than the news that tells you how to get right with God. Don't miss the boldest claim of all—**John 14:6**—where Jesus claims to be total truth.

- **Psalm 34:8** nails the point of this study. It's worth memorizing: "Taste and see that the Lord is good; blessed are those who take refuge in him."

- **James 1:22-27** says the whole point of hearing God's Word is to act on it. James says those who don't act on God's Word are like fools who look in the mirror and forget what they look like. If you live God's Word, you're wise and will experience God's blessing. Don't just jam your head with Bible facts, but practice all you know.

6. NOT JUST A GUY

Jesus is God in a human body

John 1:14

The Word became flesh and made his dwelling among us. We have seen his glory, the glory of the one and only [Son], who came from the Father, full of grace and truth.

START Most people want an unmistakably clear sign that God exists, obvious evidence of who he is. They won't be completely satisfied until they see God up close and personal. That's playing it smart, and you shouldn't settle for anything less. After all it's exactly why Jesus came to earth.

What makes you think Jesus was more than a nice religious guy? Or why might you believe otherwise?

READ John 1:1-5, 10-14

> ¹In the beginning was the Word, and the Word was with God, and the Word was God. ²He was with God in the beginning. ³Through him all things were made; without him nothing was made that has been made. ⁴In him was life, and that life was the light of all people. ⁵The light shines in the darkness, and the darkness has not overcome it.
>
> ¹⁰He was in the world, and though the world was made through him, the world did not recognize him. ¹¹He came to that which was his own, but his own did not receive him. ¹²Yet to all who did receive him, to those who believed in his name, he gave the right to become children of God— ¹³children born not of natural descent, nor of human decision or a husband's will, but born of God.
>
> ¹⁴The Word became flesh and made his dwelling among us. We have seen his glory, the glory of the one and only [Son], who came from the Father, full of grace and truth.

THINK To the people who first heard this passage, calling Jesus "the Word" meant that 1) Jesus communicates God's message; 2) Jesus is the brilliant mind that runs the universe; and 3) Jesus is God himself. Jesus is far more than an extraordinary human being; the Bible says he's been around since "the beginning." That's not a time in history but a timeless eternity. Whatever Jesus is, he's been forever.

What does it mean that Jesus is "life" and "light"?

Some people who met Jesus didn't accept these truths and rejected him. What do you think that kind of rejection looks like—then and now?

What's the result when people respond positively to Jesus?

"Receiving Jesus" means believing who he is and what he's done for you. It's how you become part of God's family forever.

LIVE Grace is God's favor or kindness we don't deserve. Truth is conformity with reality or an indisputable fact. What grace and truth do you see in Jesus?

Jesus displays God's glory—his bright, shining, majestic power. What about Jesus dazzles you?

How would you persuade a friend that Jesus shows the world who God is?

WRAP Whenever you wonder what God is like, you can spot the answer in Jesus. The Bible declares the astounding fact that, in Jesus, God became a human being and lived among us. Hebrews 1:3 says, "The Son is the radiance of God's glory and the exact representation of his being." Jesus shows you exactly who God is.

» MORE THOUGHTS TO MULL

- Christians often refer to the moment they first believed in Jesus as "receiving" or "accepting" or "trusting" him. Maybe you can point back to a moment when you received Christ. But consider this twist: How have you received Jesus *today*? How have you rejected him?

- What do you see in Jesus that changes how you think about God?

- You've "seen" Jesus in the pages of the Bible. Is that enough to satisfy you that you've seen God? Why—or why not?

» MORE SCRIPTURES TO DIG

- This passage asserts that Jesus is different from "God," yet the same. Jesus is joined together with the Holy Spirit and God the Father in a union so tight it can only be called the *Trinity*—a "tri-unity." That's difficult to grasp, but it's a teaching that runs from the front to the back of the Bible. You might be surprised that as one member of that Trinity, Jesus was indispensable to creation. **Colossians 1:16** says, "For by him all things were created: things in heaven and on earth, visible and invisible" (NIV). At the baptism of Jesus, you can spot all three members of the Trinity in one scene (**Mark 1:9-11**).

- John 1 contains one of the Bible's supreme statements about Jesus. Check a couple more in **Colossians 1:15-20** and **Hebrews 1:1-14**.

- Jesus bluntly stated that when you've seen him, you have seen God the Father. Look at **John 14:6-11**.

- Don't forget that Jesus was not only fully divine but also completely human. He had a real human body that got tired (**John 4:6**) and hungry (**Matthew 4:2**). He had human emotions like anger (**Mark 11:15-17**) and sadness (**John 11:35**). He was tempted (**Mark 1:13**). He loved (**Mark 10:21**), learned (**Luke 2:52**), and worked (**Mark 6:3**).

7. TIGHT

How to be friends with God

Colossians 1:21-22 (NCV)

At one time you were separated from God. You were his enemies in your minds, and the evil things you did were against God. But now God has made you his friends again.

START You can survive just fine with a knockoff purse. You can go wild splashing yourself with a faux fragrance. You can live happily even if your clothes are mere imitations of sought-after brand names. But when it comes to God, you want nothing fake. You need absolute authenticity. You want to be sure you've got a real relationship with the one real God.

How much does it matter to you to know—for sure—you have a genuine relationship with God? Why?

READ Colossians 1:20-23 (NCV)

> [20] And through Christ, God has brought all things back to himself again—things on earth and things in heaven. God made peace through the blood of Christ's death on the cross.
>
> [21] At one time you were separated from God. You were his enemies in your minds, and the evil things you did were against God. [22] But now God has made you his friends again. He did this through Christ's death in the body so that he might bring you into God's presence as people who are holy, with no wrong, and with nothing of which God can judge you guilty. [23] This will happen if you continue strong and sure in your faith. You must not be moved away from the hope brought to you by the Good News that you heard.

THINK What are people like before they know God? Why is that a problem?

How does God make peace with people?

Sin puts distance between people and God. Through Jesus' death on the cross we have been "brought back" or "reconciled" to God. To "reconcile" means to "reestablish a close relationship," from the word "conciliate," which means to "overcome distrust" or "to regain good will."

Describe what people are like once they have been reconciled to God through Jesus' death.

LIVE How does the Bible say you can change from being God's enemy to being God's friend?

Take another look at verses 21-23. Verse 21 says we all have a PROBLEM. Our sin separates us from God. Yet God has a SOLUTION. Jesus died in our place on the cross, suffering the punishment we deserve. And God expects a RESPONSE. He requires us to have faith, to believe what Jesus has done for us.

Belief in this "good news" isn't just "Yeah, I agree with that in my head." Having faith means you can say, "I trust my life to that." That invites an enormous question: Have you responded to God's solution to your problem with that kind of faith?

WRAP Maybe you grew up trusting that Jesus died for your sins. Perhaps you recall the particular moment when you first decided to give your life to him. Or maybe you've never responded to God's good news. If you haven't, tell God something like this: "God, I know I've wronged you. I trust that Jesus died for my sins. Thank you making me your friend, and help me live close to you." When you trust in Jesus—when you accept who he is and what he's done for you—you change from being God's enemy to being God's friend. It's how you grab hold of God's grace. And it's the first step in following Jesus.

» MORE THOUGHTS TO MULL

- Sum up in your own words the "good news" this passage talks about.

- Do you feel like God's friend? What makes you sure about your relationship with God—or unsure?

- Tell a friend how you've responded to God's solution to your problem.

» MORE SCRIPTURES TO DIG

- No one likes having their wrongdoing pointed out, much less hearing that our sin deserves punishment. But the evil things we think and do earn us death—not merely an end to our physical existence but an eternal separation from God. Jesus changes all that, because trusting in his death on our behalf allows us to be friends with God and live with him forever in heaven. **Romans 6:23** says, "For the wages of sin is death, but the gift of God is eternal life in Christ Jesus our Lord."

▪ You might worry about whether God will really forgive something you've done. Reassure yourself of God's matchless grace with **Romans 3:22**, "We are made right in God's sight when we trust in Jesus Christ to take away our sins. And we all can be saved in this same way, no matter who we are or what we have done" (NLT 1996).

▪ Read **Colossians 1:13-14** and **1:20-21** for a couple more descriptions of what it means to become God's friends.

▪ You maybe know the famous Bible verse **John 3:16**: "For God so loved the world that he gave his one and only Son, that whoever believes in him shall not perish but have eternal life." Colossians 1:21-23 is really an expanded way to say exactly how God "gave his only Son."

8. PULL TOGETHER

The feel of following Jesus

Matthew 11:29

"Take my yoke upon you and learn from me, for I am gentle and humble in heart, and you will find rest for your souls."

START Maybe you've never been closer to a cow than gulping milk from a jug that's been chilling in your fridge. But you've no doubt seen photos of old-school farming techniques where a pair of large bovines are joined side-by-side with a wooden yoke laid across their shoulders. That's the picture Jesus has in mind in this next passage. He wants you to do life attached to him.

What sounds appealing—or not—about being bound that tightly to Jesus?

READ Matthew 11:28-30

> [28]"Come to me, all you who are weary and burdened, and I will give you rest. [29]Take my yoke upon you and learn from me, for I am gentle and humble in heart, and you will find rest for your souls. [30]For my yoke is easy and my burden is light."

THINK In Luke 5:27-32 (chapter 4) you saw Jesus seeking out imperfect people, those who admit they need his help. In this scene who is he trying to recruit? What does he offer them?

The word for "weary" means being worn out from struggling or working hard. "Burdened" is more passive, like a farm animal staggering under heavy loads placed on it.

How can people find the rest Jesus offers?

What does Jesus promise about himself—and about the yoke he offers us?

LIVE The fact that Jesus promises rest isn't tough to figure out. The idea that you experience that rest by getting yoked to him might be harder to grasp. Picture this: Joining yourself to Jesus is like teaming with him to plow a field. You don't fight against him. You always go the same direction—his direction.

What do you think being yoked to Jesus looks like in everyday life?

Think of specific areas of life where you feel "weary" or "burdened." How could doing life side-by-side with Jesus help you rest?

Two questions: Are you looking for what Jesus offers? And do you believe Jesus when he says being yoked to him is "easy" and "light"? Explain.

WRAP The rest Jesus offers us is an experience completely different from what we might expect. When you stick with him—going his direction, following his teachings, tracking with him instead of going your own way—you discover Jesus doesn't aim to make you miserable. He provides deep rest. His yoke is comfortable. His expectations of you are light and life-giving.

» MORE THOUGHTS TO MULL

- How would you respond to a Christian friend who thinks that following Jesus is all about misery, hard work, toil, and sweat?

- The best rest you can get comes from doing your own thing. Agree or disagree?

- Of all the things you do to unwind, which are hollow or destructive, taking you in a different direction from Jesus?

» MORE SCRIPTURES TO DIG

- Because Jesus came to earth and lived as a human being, he knows firsthand the difficulties we face. As the Bible reports, "When he saw the crowds, he had compassion on them, because they were harassed and helpless, like sheep without a shepherd" (**Matthew 9:36**). People are "harassed," that is, bullied and oppressed. We scatter like a leaderless flock, unable to rescue ourselves or escape our tormenters. Jesus shares our pain in the deepest part of his heart.

- The kind invitation of Jesus in Matthew 11 couldn't be more different from what the crowds heard from other religious leaders. Jesus described the Pharisees like this: "They make strict rules and try to force people to obey them, but they are unwilling to help those who struggle under the weight of their rules" (**Matthew 23:4**, NCV).

- Check out this modern paraphrase of **Matthew 11:28-30**: "Are you tired? Worn out? Burned out on religion? Come to me. Get away with me and you'll recover your life. I'll show you how to take a real rest. Walk with me and work with me—watch how I do it. Learn the unforced rhythms of grace. I won't lay anything heavy or ill-fitting on you. Keep company with me and you'll learn to live freely and lightly" (MSG).

9. HAPPY ARE YOU

Upending the world

Matthew 5:8

"Blessed are the pure in heart, for they will see God."

START Jesus was no droner. He often told parables—pithy little stories or metaphors rooted in real life—that were so deep they left the crowds scratching their heads to understand them. But he also did straightforward teaching that turned his hearer's thinking upside down. The points he makes in this next passage—called the "Beatitudes"—must have left his followers dazed.

When has a teaching from Jesus challenged you—and made your head spin?

READ Matthew 5:1-12

¹Now when Jesus saw the crowds, he went up on a mountainside and sat down. His disciples came to him, ²and he began to teach them. He said:

³"Blessed are the poor in spirit, for theirs is the kingdom of heaven.

⁴Blessed are those who mourn, for they will be comforted.

⁵Blessed are the meek, for they will inherit the earth.

⁶Blessed are those who hunger and thirst for righteousness, for they will be filled.

⁷Blessed are the merciful, for they will be shown mercy.

⁸Blessed are the pure in heart, for they will see God.

⁹Blessed are the peacemakers, for they will be called children of God.

¹⁰Blessed are those who are persecuted because of righteousness, for theirs is the kingdom of heaven.

¹¹Blessed are you when people insult you, persecute you and falsely say all kinds of evil against you because of me.

¹²Rejoice and be glad, because great is your reward in heaven, for in the same way they persecuted the prophets who were before you."

THINK That word blessed might sound sweet enough to rot your teeth, but getting into the zone of God's blessing should be one of your main goals in life. Read that passage again, substituting the word happy for blessed, a solid translation as long as you remember that the biblical kind of happiness isn't a temporary fluttery feeling. It's a deep, unchanging peace.

The "poor in spirit" are the people who realize their total need for God. To be "meek" likewise means to have humility before God. Meekness remakes how you relate to people, but it doesn't make you a doormat for every cruel person in the world. To "mourn" isn't just any old sadness, but has at least partly to do with sorrow over sin. Normally we don't picture people who are beaten down—poor in spirit, meek, and mourning—as incredibly happy. But what does God guarantee these folks?

Besides the poor, meek, and mourning, who else is happy?

Jesus isn't telling you to search out sorrow or volunteer to get mangled for your faith. Yet if you truly know God, you'll find blessedness even in the midst of pain.

LIVE What benefits do you expect to enjoy from following Jesus? How does your list square with what Jesus teaches here?

Jesus says God's blessing reaches even to the tough parts of life. Are you okay with that—or do you think God should find a better way to make you happy? Explain.

WRAP Everyone knows the world has countless ways to get happy. God offers only one. He doesn't promise to make everything perfect. Yet when you do life close to him and tuck yourself into his care, he makes both good and bad times blessed.

» MORE THOUGHTS TO MULL

- Jesus' teaching in this passage flips upside down our expectations of what it takes to be happy in this world. How would you explain his words to a non-Christian friend?

- Picture a real-life situation that seems to contradict one of the points Jesus makes in the Beatitudes. How might Jesus answer your objections?

- How do you feel about the fact that part of following Jesus means digging deep into his teachings as recorded in the New Testament—and applying what you learn?

» MORE SCRIPTURES TO DIG

- Don't get the impression from the Beatitudes that God's plan for you is a life packed wall-to-wall with sorrow and wailing. Read what **James 1:17** says about God's amazing blessings: "Every good and perfect gift is from above, coming down from the Father of the heavenly lights, who does not change like shifting shadows." Or check out **Jeremiah 29:11**: "'For I know the plans I have for you,' declares the Lord, 'plans to prosper you and not to harm you, plans to give you hope and a future.'" And **1 Timothy 6:17** declares, "God richly gives us everything to enjoy" (NCV).

- The Beatitudes are just the start of a long message in **Matthew 5-7** called "the Sermon on the Mount." While it's possible that Matthew pulled together teachings from different occasions, he presents this Bible passage as a one-shot talk. The Sermon on the Mount relays some of Jesus' best-known and most practical teaching. He has strong teaching on insults and hatred (**5:21-26**), sex (**5:27-30**), divorce (**5:31-32**), revenge (**5:38-42**), loving your enemies (**5:43-48**), generosity (**6:1-4**), prayer (**6:5-15; 7:7-12**), worry and wanting too many possessions (**6:19-34**), and being a spiritual snob (**6:16-18; 7:1-6**).

- **Luke 6:20-49** makes it clear that Jesus taught on these topics more than once. Check out that passage (often called "the Sermon on the Plain") to see his emphasis on the poor and hungry.

10. WOW FACTOR

Mark 1:25-26

"Be quiet!" said Jesus sternly. **"Come out of him!"** The evil spirit shook the man violently and came out of him with a shriek.

START Throughout the Gospels—the Bible books of Matthew, Mark, Luke, and John—you can spot Jesus teaching. He schools his disciples, preaches to the crowds, and silences his critics. But he's more than a man of words. He heals the sick, tosses out demons, calms storms, feeds thousands, and even raises the dead. The multitude of supernatural episodes reported in the Gospels show that these weren't isolated events. These powerful acts made up a major part of Jesus' work.

What do you think about this supernatural side of Jesus? Would you rather picture him as a calm teacher—a guy who sports a suit and tie and steers clear of the sensational?

READ Mark 1:21-28

²¹They [Jesus and the disciples] went to Capernaum, and when the Sabbath came, Jesus went into the synagogue and began to teach. ²²The people were amazed at his teaching, because he taught them as one who had authority, not as the teachers of the law. ²³Just then a man in their synagogue who was possessed by an evil spirit cried out, ²⁴"What do you want with us, Jesus of Nazareth? Have you come to destroy us? I know who you are—the Holy One of God!"

²⁵"Be quiet!" said Jesus sternly. "Come out of him!" ²⁶The evil spirit shook the man violently and came out of him with a shriek.

²⁷The people were all so amazed that they asked each other, "What is this? A new teaching—and with authority! He even gives orders to evil spirits and they obey him." ²⁸News about him spread quickly over the whole region of Galilee.

THINK Jesus preaches and the crowd is wowed. Why?

The word for "amazed" here is strong, like getting smacked upside the head. People are astonished because Jesus doesn't have to quote other authorities to support what he says, as did the religious scholars of the time (the "teachers of the law").

As Jesus teaches, something strange happens. What? How does that interruption turn out?

Notice that the evil spirit spoke truth. First John 3:8 declares that Jesus came to destroy the power of the Devil, including the Devil's horde of "demons"— the kind of evil supernatural spirit you see here. Most Bible scholars think Jesus silences this demon so Jesus can reveal who he is in his own time. He wants to be known as more than the guy who makes demons scream.

The people praised Jesus' preaching. How do they react to his demon-tossing?

While people once again are wowed, this time their amazement is tinged with alarm. They'd never seen anything like this.

LIVE Picture this scene happening in your school and imagine how you would react. Would you be impressed, scared, puzzled—or what? How come?

The Bible teaches the supernatural world is real. It's headed by Satan, who "prowls around like a roaring lion looking for someone to devour" (1 Peter 5:8). Why does it matter to you—or not—that Jesus has power over these entities?

WRAP John 20:30-31 says Jesus performed many powerful acts, even more than were recorded in the Gospels. Yet "these are written that you may believe that Jesus is the Messiah, the Son of God, and that by believing you may have life in his name." These extraordinary events might leave you mystified. But they nevertheless signal that you follow an all-powerful Savior.

» MORE THOUGHTS TO MULL

- Do you buy the Bible's assertion that the forces of evil are real— that demons actually exist and follow a real being, Satan? Why—or why not?

- What's the big deal that Jesus doesn't teach like the "other teachers of the law"?

- What would you think of Jesus if he really did wear a white shirt, bow tie, wrinkle-free jacket, and never mixed it up with the forces of evil?

- What powerful act would you like to see Jesus do in your life?

»   MORE SCRIPTURES TO DIG

- Read this whole section, **Mark 1:21-43**, which describes a couple days in the life of Jesus. He starts off teaching in the synagogue. He tosses out a demon, heals the mother-in-law of one of his followers, and then—while he's at it—blows away hordes of demons and heals many more people.

- Don't miss what happens in the middle of these accounts. Jesus gets up "very early" by himself to pray (**Mark 1:35**). The phrase "very early" literally means "very much at night." Jesus was starting his highly public preaching and miracle-working ministry. Jesus seeks the strength that only spending time talking with his Father can provide. Look at what **Luke 5:16, 6:12**, and **9:18** say about Jesus getting away to pray.

- The Bible makes it clear that Christians have the same power over evil forces Jesus had. When you worry that evil might trash your life or even win the battle for this world, recall **1 John 4:4**: "The one who is in you is greater than the one who is in the world."

11. REAL RELIGION

John 2:15

So he made a whip out of cords, and drove all from the temple courts, both sheep and cattle; he scattered the coins of the money changers and overturned their tables.

START Ask most non-Christians why they don't follow Jesus, and close to the top of almost every list is this stinging comment: "Christians are hypocrites." Yet God is more offended by phoniness than any human being can be. If you want to spot a heated-up Jesus, just check this next passage, where he takes on religious people who aren't what they claim to be.

How do you answer the criticism that Christians are fakes?

READ John 2:13-17

> [13]When it was almost time for the Jewish Passover, Jesus went up to Jerusalem. [14]In the temple courts he found people selling cattle, sheep and doves, and others sitting at tables exchanging money. [15]So he made a whip out of cords, and drove all from the temple courts, both sheep and cattle; he scattered the coins of the money changers and overturned their tables. [16]To those who sold doves he said, "Get these out of here! Stop turning my Father's house into a market!" [17]His disciples remembered that it is written: "Zeal for your house will consume me."

THINK The opportunity to change currency for temple coins and purchase animals for sacrifice was a convenience for far-off travelers, and these practices were permitted in the outskirts of the temple. But the religious leaders had gone too far, turning the temple into a rowdy profit zone, like a concession stand at a high school football game.

Why is Jesus so enraged?

What gives Jesus the right to do a "cleansing of the temple," as this event is often called?

Remarkably, the religious leaders don't question the correctness of what Jesus did or even how he did it. They do command him to produce a sign—some proof—that he had the power to enforce God's temple rules. His response baffles them: "Destroy this temple, and I will raise it again in three days." They think he's claiming he can knock down and rebuild the stone temple that had taken half a lifetime to construct. No one realizes he's predicting his own death and resurrection (John 2:18-22).

Jesus doesn't invite his disciples to join him in the brawl. Why not?

Jesus took cleansing of his *own* house into his *own* hands, driving impostors from the temple built to honor his Father in heaven. And Jesus didn't do permanent damage. But he made a lasting statement about who he is.

LIVE What do you think of Jesus' actions against hypocritical religious leaders?

What's the difference between a religious hypocrite and an authentic follower of Jesus? Real followers never mess up, right?

How do you deal with those times when you don't live up to your own beliefs?

WRAP Jesus warned us against judging others while excusing our own sins, and he coached us to fix ourselves before we attempt to help others: "Why do you look at the speck of sawdust in someone else's eye and pay no attention to the plank in your own eye?" (Matthew 7:3). The fight against hypocrisy starts at home.

»   MORE THOUGHTS TO MULL

- Does this scene fit your picture of Jesus? Why—or why not?

- We're supposed to deal with our own sins before we talk to others about theirs. Do you think that's a subtle hint we should never help others see or escape their wrongdoing? Why—or why not?

- Is it ever right for Christians to do what Jesus did and "cleanse a temple"? When—or not?

» **MORE SCRIPTURES TO DIG**

- Jesus' tough talk against hypocrites doesn't mean his followers never mess up. In fact real Christians are the ones who admit they fail and need his forgiveness. Christians sin, but hypocrisy happens when you deny your sin and refuse to let God help you deal with it. Read **1 John 1:8—2:2** to hear God's good news for all who admit their wrongdoing.

- Jesus aims his most heated words at people who aren't what they claim to be. All of **Matthew 23**, in fact, relays his flaming judgment on the religious leaders of his day. Jesus wraps up with this: "You snakes! You brood of vipers! How will you escape being condemned to hell?" (**Matthew 23:33**).

- Dealing with your own failings while helping others deal with theirs is a delicate dance. Look for wise words on the subject in **Matthew 7:1-5** and **Galatians 6:1-5**. Note that you don't have to be perfect to help others, but God does want you to be in process with him. He wants you to be figuring out how to break free from your own sins before you worry about telling others how to escape theirs.

12. REASON TO SACRIFICE

Philippians 2:3-4

Do nothing out of selfish ambition or vain conceit. Rather, in humility value others above yourselves, not looking to your own interests but each of you to the interests of the others.

START If your idea of "servanthood" involves throwing yourself down as a doormat—so people can step on your back and scrape their shoes on your shirt—then you haven't seen servanthood the way Jesus does it. He took a bottom-rung place, but he did it by choice. He suffered brutal pain, but he did it for a reason. Even though Jesus was God himself in human form, he assumed the position of a servant. As his follower he expects you to do the same.

What motivates you to be a servant? Or what holds you back from sacrificing for others?

READ Philippians 2:1-8

¹Therefore if you have any encouragement from being united with Christ, if any comfort from his love, if any common sharing in the Spirit, if any tenderness and compassion, ²then make my joy complete by being like-minded, having the same love, being one in spirit and of one mind. ³Do nothing out of selfish ambition or vain conceit. Rather, in humility value others above yourselves, ⁴not looking to your own interests but each of you to the interests of the others.

⁵In your relationships with one another, have the same attitude of mind Christ Jesus had:

⁶Who, being in very nature God, did not consider equality with God something to be used to his own advantage;

⁷rather, he made himself nothing by taking the very nature of a servant, being made in human likeness.

⁸And being found in appearance as a human being, he humbled himself by becoming obedient to death—even death on a cross!

THINK The apostle Paul starts off with four "ifs," but the grammar makes it clear he means "of course these things are true, so then...." What all do we get from Christ, his Spirit, and one another?

Since Jesus has done all these things for us, how can we show servanthood toward other people?

Sum it up in your own words: How do the actions and attitude of Jesus give you a heart to serve?

You won't get very far in doing good to others if you don't first understand the good that God has already done for you. Seven short words in 1 John 4:19 say it well: "We love because God first loved us" (NCV).

LIVE Imagine yourself putting this passage into action in real life. What would it look like?

What's the toughest part about doing Jesus-like acts of servanthood—and having a Jesus-like attitude?

How does Jesus' servanthood toward you motivate you to serve others?

WRAP Jesus made himself nothing when he was born as a human being, then endured humankind's most merciless form of execution—all for our sake. The cross was his supreme display of servanthood and the ultimate example of the attitude God wants to build into us. Jesus didn't suffer for nothing. Everything he did was his way of displaying God's unending love for us.

» MORE THOUGHTS TO MULL

- How do high-status people usually demand to be treated? Why did Jesus choose to do the opposite?

- Who around you most faithfully lives out the principles of this passage? What can you learn from that person?

- What concrete act can you do today to put another person's interests before your own?

» MORE SCRIPTURES TO DIG

- Jesus said, "Greater love has no one than this: to lay down one's life for one's friends" (**John 15:13**). Few people ever physically die for the sake of another human being. But whenever you put yourself out for others, you're doing servanthood like Jesus did.

- Look how **Romans 12:10** gets at the heart of service: "Love each other with genuine affection, and take delight in honoring each other" (NLT).

- The early followers of Jesus had just as much difficulty with servanthood as we do. Read **Matthew 20:20-28** to see how the disciples bickered and maneuvered to gain power over one another—and what Jesus had to say about it.

- Look at **Matthew 23:12** to see the results of servanthood. And the results of pride.

- Listen to this same Bible passage in another translation to get the greatness of what Jesus did: "You must have the same attitude that Christ Jesus had. Though he was God, he did not think of equality with God as something to cling to. Instead, he gave up his divine privileges; he took the humble position of a slave and was born as a human being. When he appeared in human form, he humbled himself in obedience to God and died a criminal's death on a cross" (**Philippians 2:5-8**, NLT).

13. SOUL SATISFACTION

Who else would you follow?

John 6:68-69

Simon Peter answered him, "Lord, to whom shall we go? You have the words of eternal life. We have come to believe and to know that you are the Holy One of God."

START Once upon a time Jesus did an incredible miracle. But this was no fairy tale. He was teaching a large crowd when the time slid past mealtime. Perceiving that the crowd was restless and hungry, Jesus took a little boy's lunch of two fish and five loaves, blessed and broke them, and spread a feast to more than five thousand people. The crowd loved him so much they wanted to crown him king (John 6:1-15). But after he explained what the miracle meant, many of them wanted to ditch Jesus.

What would make you want to quit following Jesus?

READ John 6:66-69

⁶⁶From this time many of his disciples turned back and no longer followed him.

⁶⁷"You do not want to leave too, do you?" Jesus asked the Twelve.

⁶⁸Simon Peter answered him, "Lord, to whom shall we go? You have the words of eternal life. ⁶⁹We have come to believe and to know that you are the Holy One of God."

THINK Jesus fed the crowd, but he wanted them to take home more than full bellies. He expected them to digest him. He said, "I am the bread of life. Whoever comes to me will never go hungry" (John 6:35). He added, "Whoever eats my flesh and drinks my blood has eternal life" (John 6:54). When the people heard his words, they wondered, "How can this man give us his flesh to eat?" (John 6:52). Even his fans grumbled. They said, "This is a hard teaching. Who can accept it?" (John 6:60). That's when many followers turned around and went home.

What do you think Jesus means when he calls himself "bread"?

Why did people quit following Jesus? Think of at least a few reasons.

Why did Peter and the other eleven disciples decide to stay?

Jesus' inner circle had spotted at least two things in Jesus. Sure, they appreciated something he could give to them. But they also understood who he was.

LIVE What attracts you to Jesus?

How would you treat Jesus if he miraculously provided you with lunch every day—as in day after day after day?

Suppose Jesus never gave you anything but his friendship—now and for eternity. How would you feel about following him?

WRAP You'd be wide-eyed if Jesus came to your door with a pizza or two and then fed everyone in the neighborhood. But you might see him as nothing more than Jesus the Pizza Delivery Guy, a man tapped into a miraculous supply of really fine eating. Imagine your bewilderment if Jesus then declared, "I am the pizza of life." Jesus wants you to know he's the real stuff of life, everything you need to survive and thrive. He aims to be your sole satisfaction.

≫   MORE THOUGHTS TO MULL

- What all does God have to offer you? Is there anything he can't or won't give you?

- How can you focus on God the giver—not just all the good things God gives you?

- Put yourself back in that scene. Would you stay—or go? Why?

» MORE SCRIPTURES TO DIG

- Read **John 6** to catch the whole "bread of life" saga. Pay attention to all the players and how they react to Jesus. Figure out what Jesus means by "food that doesn't spoil."

- Some in the crowd surrounding Jesus that day wanted him to prove he was heaven-sent. They dared him to do another miracle, prodding him with an Old Testament episode where God provided for their forefathers by showering them day after day with an edible bread called "manna." Jesus doesn't budge. Instead of trying to top the miracle he'd already done, he simply offers them himself. Read how God miraculously fed his people with manna in **Exodus 16**.

- Jesus isn't just the bread that always satisfies. He's the water that perpetually quenches your thirst. In **John 4:10-14**, he calls himself the "living water," and in **John 7:37-39**, he declares, "Let anyone who is thirsty come to me and drink. Whoever believes in me, as Scripture has said, rivers of living water will flow from within them."

- Look at **Matthew 26:17-30** to see Jesus break bread at the "Last Supper," his last meal with his disciples before the cross—and the Bible scene that gives us our basis for the practice of Communion. Read **1 Corinthians 11:17-26** for more on the topic from the apostle Paul.

14. STEP OUT

Matthew 14:31

Immediately Jesus reached out his hand and caught him. "You of little faith," he said, "why did you doubt?"

START John 6:15 says the thousands who enjoyed a miraculous lunch with Jesus wished to propel him to the top of a political uprising. Yet Jesus had something different in mind. He sends his disciples sailing, dismisses the crowd, and slips off to pray. The Gospel of Matthew picks up the storyline and says that during the "fourth watch of the night," between 3 and 6 in the morning, Jesus set off to meet his disciples. But this was no ordinary hike. The guys see Jesus walking toward them across the Sea of Galilee. Then Peter jumps overboard to try some wave-walking for himself.

What's the most daring or difficult thing you have done for God?

READ Matthew 14:22-33

²²Immediately Jesus made the disciples get into the boat and go on ahead of him to the other side, while he dismissed the crowd. ²³After he had dismissed them, he went up on a mountainside by himself to pray. When evening came, he was there alone, ²⁴but the boat was already a considerable distance from land, buffeted by the waves because the wind was against it.

²⁵Shortly before dawn Jesus went out to them, walking on the lake. ²⁶When the disciples saw him walking on the lake, they were terrified. "It's a ghost," they said, and cried out in fear.

²⁷But Jesus immediately said to them: "Take courage! It is I. Don't be afraid."

²⁸"Lord, if it's you," Peter replied, "tell me to come to you on the water."

²⁹"Come," he said.

Then Peter got down out of the boat, walked on the water and came toward Jesus. [30]But when he saw the wind, he was afraid and, beginning to sink, cried out, "Lord, save me!"

[31]Immediately Jesus reached out his hand and caught him. "You of little faith," he said, "why did you doubt?"

[32]And when they climbed into the boat, the wind died down. [33]Then those who were in the boat worshiped him, saying, "Truly you are the Son of God."

THINK Before you conclude that the disciples were overcome by ancient superstition, ponder how you would react to someone walking toward you on the water. You too might suddenly wonder about ghosts.

Why would Peter want to walk on water?

No one is around to warn that "walking on water is only funny until someone drowns." What happens when Peter tries? How come?

Count how often "the wind" is mentioned in this passage and you realize that Jesus' disciples—several of them professional fishermen—feel real danger. Spotting Jesus walking toward them makes them feel no safer. They only feel secure when their Master climbs into the boat with them. So how do the disciples react when the wind and the waves grow still?

"Son of God" is a colossal title to bestow on Jesus. But Jesus must think the disciples don't fully understand what they're saying, because he focuses on their lack of belief. When you read the next study, watch for Jesus' reaction when Peter tries out that title again.

LIVE Put yourself back in that boat. Jesus beckons. Do you stay—or go water-walking? Why?

Why does following Jesus require moment-by-moment trust?

WRAP Jesus calls you to acts of everyday spiritual daring. The question is whether you'll take him up on his invitation to trust him in every bold move of life. Know that whatever he asks you to do, he gives you the power to do.

» MORE THOUGHTS TO MULL

- Why would Peter's lack of faith cause him to sink?

- Jesus is disappointed when his followers fail to trust him. Fair—or unfair? Explain.

- Name one way you can boldly trust Jesus today.

» MORE SCRIPTURES TO DIG

- Look at **Matthew 8:23-27**, where Jesus calms a storm that was blowing with such deadly force that the disciples questioned whether Jesus cared if they lived or died. Catch the disciples' terror along with the calmness Jesus brought to the entire scene.

- You can read another account of Jesus walking on the water in **Mark 6:47-52**, where the spiritual state of the disciples is even clearer. Their amazement at Jesus' power sounds good, but it's not. It reveals how little they actually understand about Jesus.

- The miracles of Jesus make up a substantial part of his day-in-day-out ministry. Look at just a few of his supernatural deeds. He caused a paralyzed man to walk (**Mark 2:3-12**)... healed a man born blind (**John 9:1-7**)... brought an official's son back from the brink of death (**John 4:46-54**)... calmed a storm (**Mark 4:35-40**)... caused a miraculously huge catch of fish (**Luke 5:4-11**)...cast out a legion of demons and pointed them to a bunch of pigs (**Mark 5:1-20**) ...raised a man from the dead (**John 11:1-44**)... and healed countless others of physical illness, demonization, and other afflictions.

15. WHO AM I?

Recognizing the Son of God

Matthew 16:16

Simon Peter answered, "You are the Messiah, the Son of the living God."

START Some people believe the Jesus of the Bible is nothing more than a legend. But that view ignores highly reliable points of Bible history—the acts and prophecies of God in the Old Testament; the facts of Jesus' life, death, and resurrection; and the explosive birth of the church. It ignores facts about the Bible itself, like the existence of far more evidence for the accuracy of the Bible than for other histories from the ancient world. But it's not enough to have bare facts humming around in your head about who Jesus is. It's not enough to simply read about him in a book. Jesus wants you to experience him—to know him for yourself, up close and personal.

If Jesus stood in front of you and your friends and said, "So who do *you* think I am?" what would everyone say?

READ Matthew 16:13-17

¹³When Jesus came to the region of Caesarea Philippi, he asked his disciples, "Who do people say the Son of Man is?"

¹⁴They replied, "Some say John the Baptist; others say Elijah; and still others, Jeremiah or one of the prophets."

¹⁵"But what about you?" he asked. "Who do you say I am?"

¹⁶Simon Peter answered, "You are the Messiah, the Son of the living God."

¹⁷Jesus replied, "Blessed are you, Simon son of Jonah, for this was not revealed to you by flesh and blood, but by my Father in heaven.

THINK By the time this scene occurs, it's likely that Jesus has hung out with his disciples for nearly two years. His followers have witnessed his miracles. They've pondered his sermons. They've watched him show kindness toward people who've been rejected by everyone else. Now Jesus wants to find out whether his followers really understand what they've seen.

Calling himself "the Son of Man," Jesus asks his closest followers about the word on the streets. So what's the buzz about Jesus? What do the crowds say?

Some outside of Jesus' closest friends argue that Jesus is John the Baptist— John back from the dead, that is, since he's been killed by Herod Antipas (Matthew 14:1-12). The rest think Jesus is a prophet announcing the Savior God has promised, but not the Savior himself.

Peter has been studying Jesus more closely than anyone else on earth. Who does he say Jesus is?

While the disciples no doubt had discussed the true identity of Jesus, Peter's words are a first-time, mind-boggling statement about the identity of Jesus. Possibly speaking for the group, he declares that Jesus is the chosen one come to rescue God's people. Peter recognizes that Jesus is God.

LIVE If you asked the crowds at your school or in your neighborhood who Jesus is, what would they say?

If you lived back in Bible times and had watched Jesus firsthand, what would you think about him?

That was then. This is now. So who do you say Jesus is?

WRAP The moment when the disciples finally figure out Jesus is one of the high points of the entire Bible. It also means that Jesus was on an inescapable trip to the cross: "From that time on Jesus began to explain to his disciples that he *must* go to Jerusalem and suffer many things at the hands of the elders, chief priests and teachers of the law, and that he *must* be killed...." (Matthew 16:21, italics added). But Jesus also made a bigger promise. On the third day after his death he would rise again.

» MORE THOUGHTS TO MULL

- Why does it matter what people think about Jesus, like whether they accept him as the Son of God and Savior of the world?

- Those first followers of Jesus had a lot of firsthand information about Jesus. They were also doing the tough work of figuring out his identity for the first time. Is it fair for God to expect you to reach the same conclusion about his Son? Why—or why not?

- Tell someone what you think about Jesus.

» MORE SCRIPTURES TO DIG

- In this scene we see Peter at his best—but in the very next scene, we see him at his worst. Right after Peter recognizes that Jesus is God and the Savior of the world, he openly rejects Jesus' prediction that he will go to Jerusalem and die on the cross. Jesus strongly corrects him (**Matthew 16:21-23**). Read on to see more of Peter struggling (**Matthew 26:69-75**) and growing (**John 21:15-19**).

- Now that his disciples have fully recognized him, Jesus commands them not to tell anyone what they know (**Matthew 16:20**). Just as he silenced the demon who shouted his identity (**Mark 1:21-28**), Jesus hushes his followers so he can reveal himself as he chooses. In this case the great revelation of his identity isn't far off. His death looms—but his resurrection is also ahead.

- Jesus calls himself the "Son of Man," while Peter calls him the Son of God. While you might have heard that the first title refers to Jesus' humanity and the second to his divinity, both clearly signal that Jesus is truly God. Look at **Daniel 7:13-14** to catch the "Son of Man" in action.

16. TAKE UP YOUR CROSS

Total commitment

Matthew 16:24

Then Jesus said to his disciples, "Whoever wants to be my disciple must deny themselves and take up their cross and follow me."

START If Jesus were an ordinary human being there would be a limit to what he could ask of you. Once you realize Jesus is God in human flesh—and your one-and-only Savior—it's obvious that he deserves nothing less than your whole life. The question is this: Are you going to give it to him?

Jesus not only says "Follow me!" but he explains what he means. When he says, "Hey, grab a cross!" he's inviting you to all-out commitment. So what's your reaction to that?

READ Matthew 16:24-26

> [24]Then Jesus said to his disciples, "Whoever wants to be my disciple must deny themselves and take up their cross and follow me. [25]For whoever wants to save their life will lose it, but whoever loses their life for me will find it. [26]What good will it be for you to gain the whole world, yet forfeit your soul? Or what can you give in exchange for your soul?

THINK Jesus says that anyone who wants to be his follower must do one thing. What is it? And what do you think he means?

When those first followers heard the word *cross*, they would have immediately recoiled at the thought of a violent, shameful death. They knew Jesus was demanding absolute commitment, no matter what the cost.

Brainstorm some examples from everyday life of "saving your life" or "gaining the world."

What happens if you habitually serve yourself instead of Jesus? What if you instead take up the cross and follow Jesus?

LIVE Honestly, what do you think Jesus expects of you in real life? What do "deny yourself" and "take up your cross" look like?

You can start to answer those questions by pondering what it meant for Jesus himself to take up the cross. He didn't suffer needlessly, doing hard stuff just because he enjoyed pain. He was on a mission, propelled by love to obediently follow every point of his Father's plan for him. He willingly paid an infinite price, even when it meant dying on the cross. And he didn't let anything stop him—pressing on even when others opposed him.

Why would you want to do what Jesus requires here? Before you jot down your thoughts, get a hint from Romans 12:1: "So brothers and sisters, since God has shown us great mercy, I beg you to offer your lives as a living sacrifice to him. Your offering must be only for God and pleasing to him, which is the spiritual way for you to worship" (NCV).

Look back at the primary Bible passage for this study. Is total commitment to Jesus optional—or is it Jesus' expectation of how every Christian must follow? How do you know?

WRAP These are the most challenging words Jesus ever spoke, the hardest ones to put into practice. But they also make an enormous promise: When you do life God's way, you find real life.

» MORE THOUGHTS TO MULL

- Tell Jesus what you really feel about what he says in this passage.

- Why do many Christians seem to tune out Jesus when he talks like this? More importantly, how do you usually respond to his rigorous words?

- How can you pursue this complete commitment to Jesus without looking down on other Christians who seem less passionate?

» MORE SCRIPTURES TO DIG

- If you've ever tried to follow Jesus to the utmost, you also know the feeling of being stuck right where you are. Read the rest of **Romans 12:1-2** for a giant hint about how God works in you to make you into a faithful follower: "Do not be shaped by this world; instead be changed within by a new way of thinking. Then you will be able to decide what God wants for you; you will know what is good and pleasing to him and what is perfect" (NCV). Get to know everything God has done. Let him change the way you think. And let gratitude decide what you do. Don't forget that he also promises to change you from the inside out through the Holy Spirit working inside of you (see **Romans 8** and **Galatians 5)**.

- You would think the apostle Paul would be one guy who'd have following Jesus all figured out, so he'd never fail in his attempts to obey. Check what he says in **Philippians 3:12-16**. He knows he's not perfect, but he's discovered how to get up after he's messed up.

- Matthew 16 isn't the only place where you'll find Jesus speaking about the need for our life-or-death devotion to him. You'll see similar statements in **Mark 8:34** as well as **Luke 9:23** and **14:27**. He says the same thing using different words in **John 12:23-28**.

7. ONE PATH TO PARADISE

Jesus is your one way to heaven

John 14:6

Jesus answered, "I am the way and the truth and the life. No one comes to the Father except through me."

START Only days after Jesus rose from the dead and returned to heaven, his friend Peter told the highest religious authorities of the land exactly what kind of Savior Jesus is: "There is salvation in no one else! God has given no other name under heaven by which we must be saved" (Acts 4:12, NLT). But not everyone warms to the idea that Jesus is the only path to heaven. Some outright dismiss it, while others try to reinterpret what the Bible says. You need to settle this point for yourself, because sooner or later, someone will try to talk you out of your belief.

If you asked your friends and classmates whether Jesus is really the world's one-and-only Savior—the only way to spend forever in heaven—what would they say? Explain.

READ John 14:1-6

¹"Do not let your hearts be troubled. Trust in God; trust also in me. ²My Father's house has plenty of room; if that were not so, would I have told you that I am going there to prepare a place for you? ³And if I go and prepare a place for you, I will come back and take you to be with me that you also may be where I am. ⁴You know the way to the place where I am going."

⁵Thomas said to him, "Lord, we don't know where you are going, so how can we know the way?"

⁶Jesus answered, "I am the way and the truth and the life. No one comes to the Father except through me."

THINK Jesus knows his trip to the cross is only hours away. He's already predicted that one of his closest friends will sell him out to his enemies (John 13:18-30) and that he's about to depart from his followers (John 13:33).

So in this conversation with his frightened disciples, what all does Jesus communicate?

What predicament does Thomas bring up?

Jesus provides some unexpected directions for Thomas. How will Jesus' followers get to the heavenly home he's preparing for them?

Check the words that come straight from the mouth of Jesus. What does he claim to be? How much room does he leave for an alternate route to God's home in heaven?

Notice Jesus' choice of words. He's *the...the...the....* He's not *a...a...a....*

LIVE Do you agree that Jesus is the one way to fully know God? Why—or why not?

Suppose someone says that all beliefs work equally well in helping people meet God and live in paradise forever. How would you explain what makes Christianity unique—and uniquely effective?

WRAP Plenty of wise religious teachers have been born, taught, and died. But the Bible asserts that Jesus was more than an ordinary human being. He was God come to earth. On the cross he suffered death in our place. To cap it off he rose from the dead. He's a one-of-a-kind Savior who offers you eternal life with God.

>> **MORE THOUGHTS TO MULL**

- Jesus says he is "the way," "the truth," and "the life." What do those assertions mean?

- If you could change this key part of the Christian message, would you? Why—or why not?

- Don't start a quick debate with every person on earth who disagrees with this crucial Christian message. But who needs to know what you know about Jesus? How are you planning to talk up this truth?

» MORE SCRIPTURES TO DIG

- Jesus is the only one who knows the way to the Father. He's also the only one who opened the way for you to get there. The Bible says the penalty for sin is death—not just physically dying, but being separated from God (**Romans 6:23**). And Jesus is the only person in history who died to pay for the sins of all humankind. Like **1 Timothy 2:5-6** explains, "For there is only one God and one Mediator who can reconcile God and humanity—the man Christ Jesus. He gave his life to purchase freedom for everyone" (NLT).

- Study the full accounts of Jesus' death on the cross in **Matthew 26-27, Mark 14-15, Luke 22-23**, and **John 18-19**.

- Check out **John 14:7-11** to catch more on the relationship between Jesus and his father—and why Jesus is the only one who can offer accurate directions to get home.

18. HE'S ALIVE

Walk with the risen Jesus

Luke 24:25-26

He said to them, "How foolish you are, and how slow to believe all that the prophets have spoken! Did not the Messiah have to suffer these things and then enter his glory?"

START Even though Jesus had warned his inner circle many times that he was headed for certain death on the cross, his crucifixion stunned them nevertheless. When a few female followers went to the tomb where Jesus had been buried and found it empty, their reports that he had risen seemed crazy (Luke 24:11). Yet Jesus was about to prove to all that he was truly alive. When the resurrected Jesus catches up with a couple of his followers on the road between Jerusalem and a town called Emmaus, they don't recognize him right away. He gently chides them for not comprehending his death—or his resurrection.

Suppose you were one of those early disciples who had watched Jesus be led away and executed on the cross. What would it take to convince you Jesus had risen?

READ Luke 24:25-32

[25]He [Jesus] said to them, "How foolish you are, and how slow to believe all that the prophets have spoken! [26]Did not the Messiah have to suffer these things and then enter his glory?" [27]And beginning with Moses and all the Prophets, he explained to them what was said in all the Scriptures concerning himself.

[28]As they approached the village to which they were going, Jesus continued on as if he were going farther. [29]But they urged him strongly, "Stay with us, for it is nearly evening; the day is almost over." So he went in to stay with them.

[30]When he was at the table with them, he took bread, gave thanks, broke it and began to give it to them. [31]Then their eyes were opened and they recognized him, and he disappeared from their sight. [32]They asked each other, "Were not our hearts burning within us while he talked with us on the road and opened the Scriptures to us?"

THINK Luke 24:16 says the two followers on the road "were kept from recognizing him." Scholars say the passive voice in that phrase ("were kept") indicates that God prevented them from realizing they were talking to Jesus—for a short while, anyway—while he taught them.

What does Jesus explain to these despondent followers? How does he do his explaining?

"Moses and all the Prophets" refers to Old Testament prophecies that pointed to Jesus hundreds of years before he arrived on the scene. Jump back to the end of study 2 to spot just a sampling of these many significant Scriptures.

When Jesus breaks bread the followers finally recognize their risen Lord. Again, a passive verb indicates that God himself released them to see him for who he really is. How do the travelers feel? Why?

LIVE Sum it up in your own words: Why did Jesus have to die? Why did he have to rise?

What difference does it make to your everyday life that Jesus is alive—that he's not a dead teacher locked away in an ancient tomb?

Not only is a living Savior the only kind you can relate to right here and now, but the resurrection of Jesus demonstrates he is the one-and-only Savior of the world. As Romans 1:4 says, Jesus "was shown to be the Son of God when he was raised from the dead by the power of the Holy Spirit" (NLT).

WRAP At least some of the disciples needed time to absorb all the facts about Jesus. His crucifixion? They knew that was real. His resurrection? That was tough to figure out. It took a while for that fact to sink in, but they shouldn't have been shocked. Jesus himself said it would happen: "Jesus answered them, 'Destroy this temple, and I will raise it again in three days'" (John 2:19). That's what Jesus was explaining on the road to Emmaus.

» MORE THOUGHTS TO MULL

- Why would God prevent these travelers from recognizing Jesus? Why did the disciples in general have a tough time believing Jesus was back from the dead?

- How difficult is it for you to accept the resurrection as a literal fact? Why is it tough—or not?

- Would you believe Jesus had really paid the penalty for your sins if he were still in the grave?

» MORE SCRIPTURES TO DIG

• Read the whole Emmaus road story in **Luke 24:13-32**. You can catch the Bible's resurrection accounts in **Matthew 28:1-20, Mark 16, Luke 24**, and **John 20-21**.

• Jesus predicted his death again and again in various ways. A few examples just from the book of **John**: **3:14; 7:6, 8, 30, 33-36; 8:20-21; 10:11, 15;** and **12:7, 23-24**. But he also bluntly predicted his resurrection. **Matthew 16:21** says, for example, "From that time on Jesus began telling his followers that he must go to Jerusalem, where the Jewish elders, the leading priests, and the teachers of the law would make him suffer many things. He told them he must be killed and then be raised from the dead on the third day" (NCV).

• Jesus' first appeared at the empty tomb (**Matthew 28:8-10**), then to the two travelers on the road to Emmaus (**Luke 24:13-32**). He appeared that same day to Peter in Jerusalem (**Luke 24:34**) and to ten of the disciples, all but Thomas (**John 20:19-25**). A week later he showed up for all of the disciples, including Thomas, who had doubted Jesus was really alive (**John 20:26-31**). Before Jesus headed to heaven 40 days later (**Luke 24:50-52**), he appeared to seven (**John 21:1-23**) and eleven of his disciples (**Matthew 28:16-20**), to James (**1 Corinthians 15:7**), and to more than 500 of his followers (**1 Corinthians 15:6**).

19. COME ALONG

Invite others to follow Jesus

Acts 1:8

"But you will receive power when the Holy Spirit comes on you; and you will be my witnesses in Jerusalem, and in all Judea and Samaria, and to the ends of the earth."

START Right from the start Jesus' followers have been inviting others to come along. John the Baptist, for example, encouraged two of his own followers to go after Jesus. One of them, Andrew, immediately brought his brother Simon Peter to meet Jesus. Jesus himself called Philip, who was likely a hometown friend of Andrew and Peter. When Philip realized he had found the Savior sent from God, he told his friend Nathanael. Even when Nathanael objected, he stuck to his point: "Come and see!"

Do you like to tell people that you follow Jesus—and encourage them to follow him, too? Why—or why not?

READ Acts 1:1-8

[1]In my former book, Theophilus, I wrote about all that Jesus began to do and to teach [2]until the day he was taken up to heaven, after giving instructions through the Holy Spirit to the apostles he had chosen. [3]After his suffering, he presented himself to them and gave many convincing proofs that he was alive. He appeared to them over a period of forty days and spoke about the kingdom of God. [4]On one occasion, while he was eating with them, he gave them this command: "Do not leave Jerusalem, but wait for the gift my Father promised, which you have heard me speak about. [5]For John baptized with water, but in a few days you will be baptized with the Holy Spirit."

[6]So when they met together, they asked him, "Lord, are you at this time going to restore the kingdom to Israel?"

[7]He said to them: "It is not for you to know the times or dates the Father has set by his own authority. [8]But you will receive power when the Holy Spirit comes on you; and you will be my witnesses in Jerusalem, and in all Judea and Samaria, and to the ends of the earth."

THINK That "former book" mentioned in the first verse is the Gospel of Luke. The book of Acts continues Luke's account, except that his focus now shifts to the leading followers of Jesus.

Why does Jesus tell his followers to wait in Jerusalem?

Now that Jesus has proven he's alive, what do the disciples expect him to do next?

The early disciples are still thinking like Old Testament believers, citizens of God's nation of Israel. Though Israel retains a special place in God's plans (see Romans 9-11), Jesus' focus is wider. His goal wasn't to eject the Romans who occupied Israel but to build a kingdom of followers from all around the world.

Since Jesus isn't about to start an earthly kingdom, what does he tell the disciples to do?

LIVE How intimidated are you that you're part of a worldwide plan to tell the world about Jesus?

Jesus tells his followers to start talking about him right where they are. Think of someone close to you who doesn't follow Jesus. How, when, and where could you kindly tell her or him about Jesus?

WRAP You don't have to tell the whole world about Jesus, but you can start where you are. You also don't have to have all the answers. Just begin by telling what you do know about Jesus. And why he's worth following.

» MORE THOUGHTS TO MULL

- Have you ever tried to tell someone about God—and failed miserably? What went wrong—and what would you do differently now?

- What keeps you from talking to others about Jesus? How would you answer your own objections?

- How do you know if you're saying too much about Jesus—telling someone too much too soon, more than that person can process?

»   **MORE SCRIPTURES TO DIG**

▪   Forty days after his resurrection, Jesus ascended to heaven. As his followers watched, he was "taken up," and a cloud hid him from their sight. He had come to earth on a mission to save people from their sins, and "after he had provided purification for sins, he sat down at the right hand of the Majesty in heaven" (**Hebrews 1:3**). So he's back in the throne room of God, forever on your side, living proof that your sins are forgiven (**1 John 2:1-2**). And he's promised he'll return (**Matthew 24:21-27**).

▪   "All nations" in this passage actually means "all peoples." God wants followers from every political nation, ethnic group, and language cluster. Revelation pictures "a great multitude that no one could count, from every nation, tribe, people and language" standing in front of God's throne and worshiping him (**Revelation 7:9-10**).

▪   Acts 1:8 spells out where Christians should go tell about Jesus. **Matthew 5:46-47** and **Luke 10:29-37** says who we should go to. And **1 Peter 3:15** tells us how we should speak. By the way, Acts 1:8 sounds a lot like **Matthew 28:18-20**, where Jesus spoke the "Great Commission," instructing his followers to win followers all around the world.

▪   Luke says Jesus gave "many convincing proofs he was alive" after his crucifixion. In **1 Corinthians 15:1-8**, Luke's friend Paul summarizes the times Jesus demonstrated that he was alive and well.

20. BETTER THAN ANYTHIN

Philippians 3:7-8 (NLT)

I once thought these things were valuable, but now I consider them worthless because of what Christ has done. Yes, everything else is worthless when compared with the infinite value of knowing Christ Jesus my Lord.

START The apostle Paul had lots of reasons he could feel proud—his impressive family background, stellar education, and lofty religious accomplishments. In the verses just before the passage below, he lists many of them. But then he shatters them all, arguing that they're worthless compared to one thing: Knowing Jesus.

If you asked a dozen friends and family members to identify the most important thing in your life, what would they say? What evidence could they provide?

READ Philippians 3:7-11 (NLT)

> [7] I once thought these things were valuable, but now I consider them worthless because of what Christ has done. [8] Yes, everything else is worthless when compared with the infinite value of knowing Christ Jesus my Lord. For his sake I have discarded everything else, counting it all as garbage, so that I could gain Christ [9] and become one with him. I no longer count on my own righteousness through obeying the law; rather, I become righteous through faith in Christ. For God's way of making us right with himself depends on faith. [10] I want to know Christ and experience the mighty power that raised him from the dead. I want to suffer with him, sharing in his death, [11] so that one way or another I will experience the resurrection from the dead!

THINK What do you think Paul means when he says the things he once valued are "worthless"?

There's a double meaning here. Point 1: The things Paul once thought were important are "worthless" because he had tried to use them to impress God. Now Paul knows he's acceptable to God only because Jesus died for his sins. Point 2: Those good things actually got in the way of Paul knowing Jesus. So he's putting them away, calling them "garbage." He uses a word that means "worthless trash" or even "dung."

So what does Paul most want to get out of life?

How exactly is Paul going to be accepted by God?

Paul wraps up by saying he wants to know Jesus in four deep ways: Experiencing the power that raised Jesus from the dead (God's life-changing strength), suffering with Jesus (living for him in a hostile world), sharing Jesus' death (obeying God's plans no matter what), and rising from the dead (living in heaven forever with God).

LIVE When has one of life's good things gotten in the way of you knowing Jesus better?

How much of Paul's passion do you see in your own friendship with Jesus? Explain.

What one change—large or small—could you make right now to follow Jesus more closely?

WRAP Paul's point is short and really sweet: He can't think of anything better than following Jesus. He wouldn't wish anything less for you.

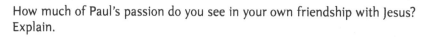 **MORE THOUGHTS TO MULL**

- Every moment of life is an opportunity to know God better. How can you make God a priority on your schedule, so you have time to focus specifically on knowing him?

- What great things about you do you count on to make you important—to God and to people? What really matters?

- How do you plan to keep getting closer to Jesus now that you've finished this book? Write yourself a promise.

» 　MORE SCRIPTURES TO DIG

- Read **Psalm 63** to glimpse what it looks like to really want to know God. Flip as well to **Psalm 84**. Then look at **Psalm 42** to see what passion for God looks like even when life isn't perfect.

- If you want to grow more in what it means to follow Jesus, watch how he follows his Father. **John 4:34** sums it up: "Jesus said, 'My food is to do what the One who sent me wants me to do and to finish his work'" (NCV).

- There's no way to show off with God, no way to score points, no way to wow him...because there's nothing you can do to earn his love. **Romans 5:8** says, "But God demonstrates his own love for us in this: While we were still sinners, Christ died for us." And **Ephesians 2:8-9** shouts, "For it is by grace you have been saved, through faith—and this not from yourselves, it is the gift of God—not by works, so that no one can boast." Your relationship with Jesus is a total gift.

www.ingramcontent.com/pod-product-compliance
Ingram Content Group UK Ltd.
Pitfield, Milton Keynes, MK11 3LW, UK
UKHW020136250325
456668UK00001B/51